Lady Gaga

D1521996

young
reader's
library of **pop
biographies**

Adele

Katy Perry

Lady Gaga

Macklemore

Nicki Minaj

young
reader's
library of **pop
biographies**

Lady Gaga

C. F. Earl

**Young Reader's Library of Pop Biographies:
Lady Gaga**

Village Earth Press
Vestal, New York 13850
www.villageearthpress.com

First Printing
9 8 7 6 5 4 3 2 1

Series ISBN (paperback): 978-1-62524-441-3
ISBN (paperback): 978-1-62524-388-1
ebook ISBN: 978-1-62524-144-3
    Library of Congress Control Number: 2014933984

Author: Earl, C. F.

Table of Contents

Chapter One

At the Top, Looking Back

At the start of the 2013 MTV Video Music Awards, all eyes were on Lady Gaga. In just a few years, the singer had become one of pop music's biggest stars. She had hit songs on radio stations across the world. She performed for thousands and thousands of fans. Gaga's albums *The Fame*, *The Fame Monster*, and *Born This Way* had sold millions of copies. At the 2013 VMAs, Gaga was ready to show fans what was next for her by performing for the first time a new song from her next album. Finally, fans who had been waiting patiently to hear new music from Lady would get to hear her latest song, "Applause."

Lady Gaga began the performance looking straight into the camera, her eyes wild as she began to sing. The camera pulled back as she sang to show Gaga in a white outfit. On her head, she wore a white square, with only her face showing.

As the song continued, Gaga began to change costumes, all while singing and dancing to "Applause." First, she went from her white dress and mask to a sparkling black bodysuit and cap. Soon, she put on a bright blue suit and blond wig. By the end of the performance, Gaga wore a seashell bikini with makeup smeared on her face. Gaga has never been afraid of wild costumes and fun fashion choices.

For Lady Gaga, music is only one part of her art. She is also ready to dress in ways that make people feel something. She uses fashion as an art form, to stir people's emotions, just as her music does. Gaga's 2013 performance of "Applause" was no different.

Today, Lady Gaga is one of the most successful women in music. Her powerful music and her exciting fashion have earned her attention from millions of fans. Gaga wasn't always the pop star fans around the world love today, though. She was once just a girl who loved music growing up in New York City.

EARLY LIFE

Before Lady Gaga took over the pop world with her big voice and bigger costumes, her name was Stefani Joanne Angelina Germanotta. Stefani was born in New York City on March 28, 1986.

Stefani's mother's name is Cynthia, but many people call her Cindy. Her father's name is Joseph. A few years after Stefani was born, her sister Natali was born.

Stefani and her family lived on the Upper West Side of Manhattan. Her parents worked hard to give their daughters a good

Lady Gaga's Style

Lady Gaga is known for her fun songs and powerful voice, but she's also known around the world for her fashion and style. Gaga rarely wears simple clothes, instead choosing incredible costumes and wild hairstyles. She's worn everything from a dress made out of raw meat to masks that cover her entire face. Gaga has performed in an outfit made of plastic bubbles and dressed as a man to perform at the 2011 MTV Video Music Awards. Gaga's fashion choices can be exciting and fun or shocking and scary, but they're never boring. Fans are always excited to see what Lady Gaga will wear to an awards show or at her next concert.

life in New York. Both Cindy and Joseph were out of the house working a lot.

While Stefani was growing up, Cindy worked at Verizon. Like Cindy, Stefani's father Joseph worked in **technology**. Years after Stefani was born, Joseph started a company that put Wi-Fi Internet connections into hotels.

Stefani and her sister went to a school in Manhattan called Convent of the Sacred Heart. Students from pre-kindergarten

Technology is anything people invent to make something easier or to do something new, such as computers and cell phones.

through twelfth grade go to the Roman Catholic girls school. Sacred Heart is one of the most expensive private schools in Manhattan. Stefani's parents worked hard to send her and her sister to one of the best schools in the city. Stefani knew how

Stefani began learning to play piano when she was just a few years old. Today, Lady Gaga plays piano at almost all of her concerts.

much her parents gave up to make sure she got the best education, so she always took school seriously.

In 2009, Lady Gaga talked to the *Minneapolis Star Tribune* about her time at Sacred Heart and how it helped make her the artist she became. "I played music every day," she told the newspaper. "Rehearsal, practice, piano. I was in plays and in bands. And I got very good grades."

Gaga continued, "I'm very, very grateful for my education. I think it's one of the things that makes me different as a pop singer."

Stefani did well in school, but things weren't always easy for her at Sacred Heart. Stefani got good grades and enjoyed learning, but she didn't feel like she fit in. Years later, Gaga talked with *New York Times* writer Nicholas Kristof about some of the bullying Gaga experienced in high school.

"I was called really horrible, profane names very loudly in front of huge crowds of people, and my schoolwork suffered at one point," Gaga told Kristof about her time in school. "I didn't want to go to class. And I was a straight-A student, so there was a certain point in my high school years where I just couldn't even focus on class because I was so embarrassed all the time. I was so ashamed of who I was."

In high school, Stefani was thrown into a trashcan by some boys who lived down her street who were making fun of her. She has talked about how hurt she felt by the way other kids her age picked on her.

While Stefani had a hard time because of bullying, she also learned a lot about music that would shape her future. Even though she didn't always feel confident in school, Stefani found confidence in music and acting.

Stefani did well at Sacred Heart, but she also had a hard time fitting in at the New York City private school, shown here.

STEFANI ON STAGE

From an early age, Stefani always loved music and performing for other people. Gaga remembered one of her first musical memories for *Harper's Bazaar* magazine in early 2014, telling the magazine, "I went to see *Phantom of the Opera* with my grandma and my mom when I was very little. The stage, the voice, the music?... Composer Andrew Lloyd Webber has been a massive **inspiration** to me for some time—the storytelling, that deliciously **somber** undertone in his music. I just knew that he could see it while he was creating it," Gaga told the magazine. "It is the same way I experience music."

Stefani began playing piano when she was just a few years old. She started writing her own songs when she was a young teenager. Gaga told *New York* magazine about playing piano at Sacred Heart when she was just eight years old. "There was a line of twenty girls sitting in a row in our pretty dresses, and we each got up to play. I did a really good job. I was quite good."

Stefani also loved acting. When she was eleven, she started taking acting classes on Saturdays. She told *New York* magazine that she remembers learning to drink out of an imaginary coffee cup. "That's the very first thing they teach you. I can feel the rain, too, when it's not raining." She learned that experiencing things that weren't really there was an important piece of acting.

Stefani began acting in plays in her high school. She got the lead in *Guys and Dolls* and *A Funny Thing Happened on the Way to the Forum*, she told *New York* magazine. On stage, Stefani was confident and happy. She loved to perform, whether she was singing in a school musical or playing piano. After high school, Stefani would take her talents to a whole new level.

Find Out Even More

When you want to learn more about the musicians and singers you love, reading books at your library is a great way to start. A book about one person's real life is called a biography. If someone writes a book about his or her own life, it's called an autobiography. Reading biographies and autobiographies is one of the best ways to learn about the music you love and the people who make it.

While reading biographies is a great way to get new facts and stories about music's biggest stars, no one biography can tell the whole story. To get the best view of a singer's life, you'll have to read more than one biography. Even in an autobiography, the singer or musician writing about their life may leave certain facts out. They may forget things over time or want to keep some stories private. Writers working on biographies have to pick which facts to put in the book, and which to leave out. Reading many books about the topics you love is always the best way to get the most information.

Try finding some of the Lady Gaga biographies below:

Heos, Bridget. *Lady Gaga (Megastars)*. New York: Rosen Publishing Group, 2011.

Krumenauer, Heidi. *Lady Gaga (Blue Banner Biographies)*. Hockessin, DE: Mitchell Lane Publishers, 2010.

Tieck, Sarah. *Lady Gaga: Singing Sensation (Big Buddy Biographies)*. Minneapolis, MN: Abdo Publishing, 2011.

Take a look through one of the books you've found and think about the following questions:

1. Look at the table of contents and find a chapter that sounds interesting to you. Flip to the chapter and read a few pages. Did the chapter title help you to know what the chapter would be about and quickly find information you wanted to know?
2. How is the biography organized? Many biographies tell the story of a person's life from beginning to end. Others may use another structure. How does this biography organize Lady Gaga's life story to make it easy to understand?
3. Does the book have an index? Look over the index and try to find topics that interest you. Using the index, find those topics and read a bit about whatever you've chosen.
4. Do you like the book? Why or why not? Is there information in this book that you don't think you could find in another biography you found?

Chapter Two

Stefani Becomes Lady Gaga

After graduating from Sacred Heart, Stefani started taking classes in theatre at New York University. She was accepted into the Collaborative Arts Project 21 (CAP21) at New York University's Tisch School of the Arts, a famous school for actors, directors, and filmmakers. Stefani was only seventeen years old when she moved into an NYU dormitory and started working to become an actor.

Though she enjoyed acting, Stefani soon realized that music was her true **passion**. She quit CAP21 when she

> Your **passion** is something you care strongly about.

was nineteen. Her father offered to help her pay for a place to live in New York while she worked on her music career. In 2005, Stefani found an apartment in the city and began working to make it in music. Her father told her that he'd help her for a year, but after that she'd have to pay for her apartment on her own and find another job.

STARTING IN MUSIC

Stefani started a band called The Stefani Germanotta Band (also called SGBand) and began playing shows around New York. She sang both original songs she wrote and famous rock-and-roll songs. Stefani worked hard, but she didn't find much success with SGBand at first. Then, just a short time before her year of help from her father was over, Stefani and her band played a show where Wendy Starland, another singer, noticed Stefani had something special. Wendy told music **producer** Rob Fusari about Stefani's performance and her amazing voice. Rob had made hits for artists like Destiny's Child and Will Smith. Wendy told Rob he should start working with Stefani.

SGBand split up, and Stefani started writing songs with Rob and recording her own music. She traveled to New Jersey every day for weeks to record with Rob. The two became close friends while working together.

A music **producer** is in charge of recording a piece of music and making it into a final product.

Rob helped Stefani come up with a new name that she would go on to make famous. Stefani and Rob always loved the song "Radio Ga Ga" by rock band Queen. Rob said that he would play the song for Stefani as a sort of theme song. One day, Rob was joking with Stefani in a text message when the phone corrected "Radio Ga Ga" to "Lady Gaga." Stefani said that she knew right away that Lady Gaga would be her new name from then on.

In 2006, Gaga thought she'd found a way to reach her musical dreams when she got a record contract with Def Jam Records. Soon, the **label** told her, she would have the chance to put out an album. It wasn't long before the label stopped working with Lady Gaga, however, just a few months after giving her a record deal and promising to put out her music. She was dropped from Def Jam. Gaga was crushed. She had come so close to her dreams, only to have the people who promised her so much take it all away.

Gaga returned to New York feeling like she might never make it in music. She started going out at night and singing in downtown New York clubs while living at home. At the same time, she began experimenting with performing in wild costumes, or even almost no clothes at all. Although she was sad during this time, she was also becoming more and more like the Lady Gaga fans know today. She was letting herself be different.

Gaga met Lady Starlight performing and partying around New York. The two began working on music shows together, performing as "Lady Gaga and the Starlight Revue." The show started to get the pair noticed. They even performed at Lollapalooza, a giant music festival, in front of hundreds and hundreds of music fans.

In 2007, the music Gaga made with Rob Fusari made its way to

A **label** is a company that publishes music.

Gaga performs for new fans in 2008.

Vincent Herbert. Vincent is an **executive** at Interscope Records, one of the biggest record labels in the world. He wanted to start a new smaller label at In-

terscope called Streamline Records. He signed Lady Gaga to the new label and gave her the chance to get her first music under her new name out to music fans everywhere.

THE FAME

Lady Gaga put out her first album, *The Fame*, in August 2008. Even with big hit songs like "Just Dance," "Poker Face," "LoveGame," and "Paparazzi," though, the album didn't became a top seller right away. When the album came out, it sold 24,000 copies. Over the next few months, however, more people heard songs like "Just Dance," and "Poker Face" on the radio and watched videos online. By early 2009, *The Fame* broke into the top ten on the *Billboard* album charts. In the five years after the album's release, *The Fame* sold almost 5 million copies. *The Fame* had a slow start, but it proved to be a huge success for Gaga.

Gaga created some amazing music for the album. "Just Dance" took a few months to become a number-one hit on the *Billboard* Hot 100 chart, but the song was one of Gaga's first hits. She spoke to ArtistDirect.com about why the song became so popular. "I think that everyone is looking for a song that really speaks to the joy in our souls and in our hearts and having

Music History: The *Billboard* Charts

In 1984, *Billboard* magazine began printing information about the latest entertainment of the time. Years later, the magazine focused almost entirely on music. In the 1930s, *Billboard* began keeping track of the best-selling and most-popular songs and musical artists. Today, each kind of music—from rock to hip-hop, from pop to electronic dance music—has it's own chart, tracking the popularity of songs and albums. Artists watch the charts closely, hoping to get a number-one song or album. For many artists, having a song top the *Billboard* charts is the highest mark of success in the music business. Today, the Hot 100 chart is the most important pop music chart, keeping track of the biggest hits in music.

a good time. It's just one of those records. It feels really good, and when you listen to it, it makes you feel good inside. It's as simple as that," she told the website.

"Poker Face" also reached the number-one spot on the Hot 100 chart. Gaga put out her next single "Eh Eh (Nothing Else I Can Say)" after "Poker Face," and though the song wasn't as big a hit as her first two singles, it was still a huge hit for Gaga in countries around the world. Fourth single "Paparazzi" and "LoveGame" were hits as well.

Music History: The Grammy Awards

The Grammys are one of music's biggest awards. Each year, the Recording Academy presents the Grammys to give people in the music business a chance to vote on the year's best music. First given out in 1959, the Grammys have been around for more than 50 years. For more information about the Grammy Awards, visit www.grammy.com.

At the 2009 Grammy Awards, Lady Gaga won her first Grammys. "Poker Face" won for Best Dance Recording while *The Fame* won for Best Electronic/Dance Album.

With *The Fame*, Gaga had become a music star, with hit songs on the radio and videos seen by millions. Her music reached so many people and gained her millions of fans, something many artists can only dream of. Stefani Germanotta had gone from feeling insecure at school to having her face and voice everywhere.

After the success of Lady Gaga's first album, the singer began to travel the world to perform for her fans. Gaga called her first tour The Fame Ball Tour. She performed for fans in Europe, Australia, and Asia. Thousands of fans got to see Gaga's incredible show. She wanted to bring fans into her world of art and music and fun. Gaga changed costumes, played instruments, and played characters during a single performance. The tour, like the album, was a huge success.

Find Out Even More

Finding books at your school library is a great way to learn more about the music and artists you find interesting. Going online is another great way to find out information about the music you listen to.

Search engines are usually the best place to start looking for facts about people like Lady Gaga online. There is no limit to the amount of information you can find on the Internet. Search engines help you sort through all of the information to bring you the best, newest, or most popular results.

To use search engines like Google.com or Bing.com for facts or articles about Lady Gaga, you'll have to use keywords. Keywords are the words you type into the search bar to find what you're looking for. Making sure you choose the right key words is an important part of researching your favorite music online. Use the wrong keyword or misspell your keywords, and you probably won't find just what you're looking for.

Try searching for some of the keywords on the next page to find out more about important parts of Lady Gaga's early life and career:

Convent of the Sacred Heart
Collaborative Arts Project 21 (CAP21)
Vincent Herbert
The Fame
Billboard album chart history

Chapter Three

Fame and Little Monsters

With *The Fame*, Gaga went from a struggling singer to a superstar. But her rise to the top of music wasn't finished yet. Near the end of 2009, she released her second album *The Fame Monster*. At first, *The Fame Monster* was planned as a new version of Gaga's first album. Instead, the album included eight new songs, including songs that would become some of the singer's biggest hits.

THE FAME MONSTER

After the success of her first album, *The Fame*, she had millions of fans waiting to hear new music from their favorite new pop star. Gaga didn't disappoint them. The first single from *The Fame Monster* was "Bad Romance." The heavy dance beat and amazing singing from Gaga made the song a huge hit. "Bad Romance" reached number two on the *Billboard* Hot 100 chart, making it her biggest hit since "Poker Face" and "Just Dance."

Lady Gaga arrives at the 2010 MTV Video Music Awards in her dress made of raw beef.

"Bad Romance" was **nominated** for Best Pop Video at the 2010 MTV Video Music Awards. When Lady Gaga went to the award show, she wore a dress, shoes, and a hat that were all made of raw meat.

When you are **nominated** for an award, you are in the running to win it.

Venues are places where a performance takes place.

The meat dress shocked many people and got others talking. It's one of Gaga's wildest and most unforgettable fashion choices.

The Fame Monster also had other hits. "Alejandro" and "Telephone" were two of the biggest songs from the album. Beyoncé sings with Lady Gaga on "Telephone" and the two filmed a video for the song together. Lady Gaga also worked with the superstar singer on Beyoncé's song "Video Phone."

The Fame Monster sold hundreds of thousands of copies in its first few weeks. By the beginning of 2010, more than a million fans bought the album. At the 2010 Grammys, Gaga's new album won Best Pop Vocal Album. "Bad Romance" won an award for Best Female Pop Vocal Performance. The song's video also won an award, and Gaga performed with Elton John during the show. In just a few years, she had won five Grammy Awards, while many artists work for their entire lives to win just one!

Just as she had after *The Fame* came out, Lady Gaga began a tour after the release of *The Fame Monster*. She called her new tour The Monster Ball Tour. Again, she performed for fans around the world.

One of the **venues** on her tour was Madison Square Garden in New York City. For years, performing at large arena has been a sign of an artist's popularity and success—and Madison Square Garden is one of the most famous places to perform in the world. Gaga followed up the concert with a DVD of her performance called *Lady Gaga Presents the Monster Ball Tour: At Madison Square Garden.*

At the time of the Monster Ball Tour, Lady Gaga was already one of the biggest stars in music just a few years into her music career. She come a long way very quickly! And by 2011, Lady Gaga was ready to give her fans new music.

BORN THIS WAY

At the 2011 Grammy Awards show in February, Lady Gaga again startled the world: she arrived on the red carpet in an egg. Four people carried her into the Staples Center in Los Angeles before the show. Gaga later told fans she had spent days in the egg before her performance that night. She said she wanted to be born again on stage.

That night Gaga performed her new song "Born This Way" for the first time. Soon, Gaga released an album with the same name. *Born This Way* had an important message from the singer. Gaga talked to Time Out London about her inspiration for some of the ideas on *Born This Way.* "Being bullied stays with you your whole life, and no matter how many people are screaming your name or how many Number One hits you have, you can still wake up and feel like a loser,' she told the magazine.

"Those people who feel bullied or like nerds," she went on, "I'm trying to make them feel like winners, but I'm not trying to make them hate all of the cool kids more. It's all about closing

Lady Gaga's Little Monsters

Many pop stars have names for their fans. Nicki Minaj calls her fans "barbz." Beyoncé's fans are part of the "Bey Hive." Lady Gaga calls her fans "Little Monsters" and many fans call Gaga "Mother Monster." Gaga's bond with her fans goes far beyond music. Gaga often speaks about the love she has for her little monsters. She says her fans inspire her and she hopes she can inspire them. Lady Gaga even started a website called Littlemonsters.com for her fans to meet and talk online.

the gap and bringing people closer together. And that's what the pop end of my music is all about.'

Gaga's *Born This Way* was another huge success for the pop star. The album sold more than a million copies in the first week. In the three years after the album's release, more than two million fans bought *Born This Way*.

The single "Born This Way" became a number-one hit right away. Many people saw Gaga's amazing Grammy performance, and they loved her new song. Fans also liked the song's message: it's okay to be who you are. The album *Born This Way* also featured other hits like "The Edge of Glory" and "Marry the Night."

In August, Gaga performed at the 2011 MTV Video Music Awards. She turned her performance into another unforgettable

Gaga poses as Jo Calderone with her new MTV Video Music Awards after the 2011 awards show.

moment. Gaga took the stage as Jo Calderone, her male **alter ego**, a man dressed in a black suit and white t-shirt. Many people didn't know what to think, but Gaga's fans loved the performance.

In 2012, Lady Gaga started her Born This Way Ball Tour. She performed in nations around the world for almost a year before she had to stop the tour because of an accident. Gaga fell and hurt her hip. She couldn't walk, let alone perform. She needed surgery to get better, she but felt awful for having to cancel shows. She told fans she had even tried to keep the truth about how badly she was hurt from people close to her. "I didn't want to disappoint my amazing fans," Gaga wrote on Twitter. Though many people were sad to hear about the canceled concerts, most of Gaga's closest fans sent her get-well wishes and hoped to hear from Mother Monster again soon.

An **alter ego** is a second, different personality from whom you usually are.

Find Out Even More

When you're using search engines to find information about your favorite music, Wikipedia is often one of the first search results. The online encyclopedia can be a good place to start finding out more about an artist, album, or song. But it's important to remember a few key things about Wikipedia.

First, all the information on Wikipedia is posted by the website's users. This means that there is usually a lot of information on the site about a lot of different topics. But not all of the information posted is good. Not all the facts on Wikipedia are true. Knowing that what you read on Wikipedia can come from almost anyone means that you have to check the facts on the website.

The best facts on Wikipedia have a source. To read the article or interview that's the source for a particular fact is the best way to make sure what you're reading is good information. To find the fact's source, look for a small number at the end of the sentence you're reading. Clicking on that number will bring up the name of and a link for the source article. You can click on the link and read the source for the fact you're checking. Good facts on Wikipedia are linked to sources. Always make sure to check for the source when you're not sure about something you're reading on the online encyclopedia.

Wikipedia has information about a huge number of topics. It can be a great way to find a little bit of information about a lot of different things. But Wikipedia usually isn't the best source of information. Reading Wikipedia might be a good way to start your search for information, but you'll need other sources—like other websites or books—when you're looking for information about the artists and music you love.

Chapter Four

Born to Perform

After the amazing success of Lady Gaga's *Born This Way*, the pop singer was ready to return with new music in 2013. Soon, Gaga would show all of her fans *Artpop*, her third album.

GAGA'S *ARTPOP*

Gaga talked about how she had a hard time recovering from her hip surgery. She had been depressed she told fans. But *Artpop* was also about confidence and feeling sure of herself as an artist and musician. Before *Artpop* came out, Gaga told *Glamour* magazine about the confidence she felt about the new album and her costume-changing performance of "Applause" at the 2013 MTV VMAs.

"I'm confident in who I am," she told the magazine. "I've come to a place in my life where I've accepted things that are me, as opposed to feeling pressure to explain myself to people around me. That's just the way I've always tried to be," Gaga said. "It didn't change when I became a star."

Artpop was another successful album for Gaga. The album didn't sell as much as *Born This Way* when it came out, but more than 250,000 fans bought *Artpop* in its first week. The album came out at number-one on *Billboard*'s album chart. Dance songs "Applause" and "Do What U Want" (a song with singer R. Kelly) were huge hits.

Throughout 2014, Gaga toured the world again. She called her new tour ArtRave: The Artpop Ball. As with all of Lady Gaga's tours, she performed in different costumes and made her show a night for fans to remember.

Gaga has hinted that *Artpop* might just be the first of two parts. She's said she might put out a "Act 2" for *Artpop*. If she does, her fans are sure to be waiting for new music from the superstar.

MORE THAN MUSIC

Lady Gaga has had amazing success in music since she began her career. But she's also done incredible things in business and spoken out about many issues that are important to her. Gaga is much more than a musician and singer. She's a businessperson and an **activist** for causes close to her heart.

Gaga has partnered with huge companies like Polaroid, H&M, and Armani. She also created her own perfume line. She's working with a company called Backplane to create online social communities for herself and other music artists where fans can chat online and talk about their favorite music. Lady Gaga may have gotten her start in music, but she's made a name for herself in business as well.

Gaga has also worked hard to fight for causes that she thinks are important. She's spoken out against bullying online and given speeches supporting **LGBT** rights. Gaga believes love between two people is the most important thing in the

Born This Way Foundation

In 2012, Lady Gaga started the Born This Way Foundation (BTWF). The foundation was founded to fight for acceptance of others and against bullying, online or in schools. On the BTWF website (www.bornthiswayfoundation.org), the foundation says it is "dedicated to creating a safe community that helps connect young people with the skills and opportunities they need to build a kinder, braver world." The foundation's website also says, "We believe that everyone has the right to feel safe, to be empowered and to make a difference in the world. Together, we will move towards acceptance, bravery and love." The Born This Way Foundation is just one way Lady Gaga is giving back to her fans and working to change the world for the better.

world—whether between two women, two men, or a man and a woman. She has spoken passionately in favor of gay marriage many times.

LOOKING TO THE FUTURE

Today, Lady Gaga is one of the most famous people making music. She's sold millions of albums and performed for huge audiences around the world. People around the

An **activist** is someone working to change the world for the better.

LGBT refers to lesbian, gay, bisexual, and transgender people, their community, and their political rights.

Gaga spoke out in 2010 against Don't Ask, Don't Tell, a rule that kept LGBT people from serving openly in the United States military.

world know her name, her **lyrics**, and her most famous looks. Gaga's costumes and fashion have created amazing moments, shocked people, and made fans around the world start talking about Mother Monster. Many people make pop music, but there is only one Lady Gaga.

She may be a megastar today, but before there was Lady Gaga, there was Stefani Germanotta, a high school student who was unsure of herself, hoping to fit in and feel loved. She was bullied and felt shame about being herself. Through music and art, however, Stefani transformed her life and became Lady Gaga. She overcame her lack of self-confidence and changed her life. She's proven to adolescents around the world what is possible when you use all your **creativity** to do something amazing, when you dare to be true to yourself.

For all her success, Gaga always tells her fans that she's just like them. Even as a famous singer she feels doubt about her-self. She still has struggles with self-confidence. Shy Stefani still lives somewhere inside the Lady Gaga super-star. But she also knows that being herself is the best way to be. She knows that performing her songs the way she wants to perform them—and wearing what she wants to wear—is the best way to express herself. Gaga is fearless in her music and art, even when Stefani may feel unsure.

Lady Gaga told CNN talk show host Larry King about what she wants to do with her art and music. "I'm…interested in helping my fans to love who they are," she told Larry, "and helping them to reject **prejudice** and reject those things that they're taught from **society** to not like themselves, to feel like freaks, that they're not wanted."

Lyrics are the words of a song.

Creativity is the ability to come up with new ideas.

Prejudice is making judgments about people before you really know them.

Society is made up of people living together in an organized way.

An **icon** is a person who represents something bigger than herself.

To millions of people around the world, Lady Gaga is a pop **icon** with a purpose. She makes music and art to show her fans that they can be themselves—whether they want to wear a dress made of meat or sing about how they feel. And her fans—her little monsters—are always ready to hear what she has to say next, see what she's wearing, and hear her new music.

Find Out Even More

Today, many artists use Facebook and Twitter to talk to their fans. Lady Gaga has her own Twitter and Facebook accounts. With social media websites like these, she sends messages out to the millions of people who listen to her music online.

If you're looking for information about what's happening right now with Lady Gaga (whether she's touring or has new music coming out, for instance), social media can be a good place to learn more. But not everything you read on social media is good information. Sites like Facebook or Twitter are filled with many peoples' opinions. You can't always be sure what you're reading is good information on social media websites about an artist like Lady Gaga unless it comes directly from her.

On Twitter, you can make sure you're getting information from Mother Monster herself by checking for the verified account mark on her Twitter page. If an artist's page has a blue check mark on it, you know that Twitter has "verified" their account. That means the company's made sure to check to see that the account is run by Lady Gaga herself and the messages posted to her Twitter page come from her.

On Facebook, make sure you're visiting an artist's official page to be sure you're getting messages straight from the artist. A fan may set up a Facebook page that doesn't post solid information you can trust. The official page for a band or artist is only going to post accurate information about tour dates, new music, or new videos.

Social media is a big part of the Internet and it can be a great place to find out new information about your favorite music. But always remember that the Internet allows people to voice their own thoughts and opinions— and people can post things that aren't true. It can be fun to be part of the conversation, but don't forget to check facts by looking at news websites, reading interviews, or checking out biographies at your library.

Here's What We Recommend

IN BOOKS

Aloian, Molly. *Lady Gaga (Superstars!)*. New York: Crabtree Publishing Company, 2011.

Edwards, Posy. *Lady Gaga: Me & You*. London, UK: Orion Publishing Group, 2010.

Frisch, Aaron. *Lady Gaga (Big Time)*. Mankato, MN: The Creative Company, 2013.

Yasuda, Anita. *Lady Gaga (Remarkable People)*. New York: Weigl Publishers, 2012.

ONLINE

Lady Gaga's Official Website
www.ladygaga.com

Lady Gaga's Official Twitter (@ladygaga)
twitter.com/ladygaga

Lady Gaga on *Billboard*.com
www.*Billboard*.com/artist/306341/lady-gaga

Lady Gaga on Grammy.com
www.grammy.com/artist/lady-gaga

Lady Gaga on MTV.com
www.mtv.com/artists/lady-gaga

Index

About the Author

C.F. Earl is a writer living and working in Binghamton, New York. Earl writes on a range of topics, including pop culture, history, and health.

Picture Credits

Made in United States
Orlando, FL
12 September 2024

51461889R00029